Martina,
Hopefully this books
brings back some of
wonderful memories of
your trip. Happy Birthday.

NEW YORK CITY

WHITECAP BOOKS
VANCOUVER / TORONTO / NEW YORK

Text by Tanya Lloyd
Edited by Elaine Jones
Photo editing by Tanya Lloyd
Proofread by Lisa Collins
Cover and interior design by Steve Penner
Desktop publishing by Roberta Batchelor
Printed and bound in Canada

Canadian Cataloguing in Publication Data

Lloyd, Tanya, 1973–

New York City

(America Series)
ISBN 1-55285-113-3

1. New York (N.Y.)—Pictorial works. I. Title. II. Series: Lloyd,
Tanya, 1973- America series.
F128.37.L66 2000   974.7'1044'0222   C00-0911069-0

The publisher acknowledges the support of the Canada Council and the Cultural
Services Branch of the Government of British Columbia in making this publication
possible. We acknowledge the financial support of the Government of Canada through
the Book Publishing Industry Development Program for our publishing activities.

**For more information on the America Series and other Whitecap Books
titles, please visit our web site at www.whitecap.ca.**

Gazing at the New York City skyline—the sun reflecting from the Chrysler Building, the sweep of the Brooklyn Bridge—it's hard to imagine that this was once a tobacco plantation. But that's exactly what the Dutch settlers envisioned when they arrived in the 1600s. Leader Peter Minuit bought the land from the Algonquin people, entrepreneurs began harvesting timber, and soon New Amsterdam was a thriving colony.

When England gained control in the latter part of the century, Charles II renamed the area New York. That title remained, even after George Washington led the American troops to independence. The British surrendered New York in 1783; two years later it was the capital of the newly born United States.

Though no longer the capital of the nation, the New York of today is often called the capital of the world. The bustling streets of Manhattan and the boroughs of the Bronx, Brooklyn, Queens, and Staten Island are home to residents of every possible heritage—many descended from those who arrived at Ellis Island centuries ago. Buildings echoing the styles of historic Hong Kong or Florence stand only blocks from spectacular skyscrapers and innovative examples of modern architecture. The flags of the world wave before the United Nations headquarters, while goods from countless countries are bought and sold in the offices of the Financial District.

High finance aside, this is an undisputed cultural capital. The box offices of the New York City Ballet, the New York City Opera, and the Philharmonic compete with Broadway plays and live television shows for audiences. From buskers to virtuosos, the streets offer every kind of performance, an array to appeal to even New York's diverse population.

With 150 museums, 10,000 shops, and more than 18,000 restaurants serving every possible variety of food, it's no wonder New York City draws millions of visitors.

The four glass and granite towers in Battery Park City are collectively known as the World Financial Center and house the head offices of some of the world's best-known corporations, including American Express, Merrill Lynch, and Dow Jones.

Open courtyards and gardens, 50 shops and restaurants, and a wide-ranging arts program sponsored by the buildings' high-profile tenants make the World Financial Center an inviting place to visit. More than two million people have attended performances here since the arts program began in 1998.

The New York Stock Exchange owes its distinctive pediment to sculptor John Quincy Adams Ward. Ward's stylized figures symbolize areas of American commerce, including agriculture, mining, and invention. The central figure represents integrity.

Built on landfill—much of it created when the World Financial Center towers were built—Battery Park City encompasses 92 acres. As well as upscale residences, the neighborhood boasts an extensive esplanade and five public parks.

Almost two million people a year visit the hundredth floor of the World Trade Center. At more than 1,000 feet, the promenade there is the highest outdoor observation deck in the world. For those who don't care to scale the heights, the center also offers the city's largest indoor shopping mall.

The twin towers of the
World Trade Center soar
1,350 feet, making them
the city's tallest buildings.
They were designed by
Minoru Yamasaki in the
1960s as part of a plan by
the Port Authority of New
York and New Jersey to
increase international
commerce.

The heart of shipping activities in the mid-1800s, the South Street Seaport was home to sailmakers and saloons, boarding houses and brothels, all catering to the thousands of sailors who arrived here each year. Today, this is a favorite after-work destination for Wall Street workers.

The South Street Seaport fell into disuse in the late 1880s, when the
shipping industry outgrew the site. The area was reborn in 1967
with the opening of the South Street Seaport Maritime Museum.
Restored buildings and a picturesque boardwalk now line the water.

Created by Cass Gilbert, the Woolworth Building (pictured on the left) was the world's tallest for 17 years and shows the designer's love of the neo-gothic style. The tower took more than a year to build, and was completed in 1913.

Visitors take a boat cruise through New York Harbor for a unique perspective on the Statue of Liberty and Manhattan Island. These waters were first explored by Giovanni da Verrazano, an Italian-born navigator commissioned by France to seek a passage through North America to the Pacific.

The Statue of Liberty, a
gift to the United States
from the people of France,
was dedicated in 1886
and remains a symbol of
freedom. Standing more
than 300 feet tall from
foundation to torch, the
statue weighs more than
225 tons, and draws five
million visitors each year.

The Ellis Island Museum explores the history of immigration in the United States and the world. Only 2 percent of the steerage and third-class passengers who arrived at Ellis Island were refused entry into the United States, but their stories were enough to earn it the title Island of Tears.

Now restored and protected as part of the Statue of Liberty National Monument, Ellis Island was the debarkation point for about 12 million people between 1892 and 1954. Forty percent of the nation's population is descended from these immigrants.

Designed by John
Roebling between
1867 and 1883, the
Brooklyn Bridge was
the first suspension
bridge to be made
of steel. The use of
thick steel cables,
strung between the
bridge's signature
arches, allowed it
to span a greater
distance than any
previous suspension
bridge.

A tiny corner of Lower Manhattan, Chinatown is home to about a third of the city's Chinese population. The population gets a boost each evening, when thousands of visitors flock here to sample the specialties of more than 300 restaurants.

From traditional medicines and Asian produce to tea services and hand-painted screens, the crowded shops of Chinatown offer an array of authentic cultural wares.

Tattoos, body piercings, wigs, and alternative clothing—the East Village has retained its bohemian atmosphere as the nearby West Village has become more upscale. This is the perfect place to find the wild and the offbeat, or just to window shop or people watch.

SoHo—named for its location south of Houston Street—was a warehouse district in the nineteenth century. It became one of the city's worst slums, known as "hell's hundred acres," but by the 1960s artists had reclaimed the warehouses as galleries and loft residences. This is now one of New York's trendiest neighborhoods.

Once the site of a Dutch tobacco plantation, then a collection of residential estates, Greenwich Village was named by Sir Peter Warren, an English fleet commander who lived here with his family after the British won control of New Amsterdam in 1664.

Coffeehouses and cafés are still central to life in Greenwich Village. Jazz filters onto the streets and urbanites wander the sidewalks until late in the evenings.

The townhouses surrounding Washington Square were built by thriving merchants in the 1850s. By the mid-1900s, the buildings were inexpensive enough for artists and intellectuals, and Greenwich's reputation as a bohemian village was born.

Chess players match wits in Washington Square, perhaps drawing inspiration from the great minds who populated the village in the past. Edgar Allen Poe wrote *The Raven* here, Henry James lived at 1 Washington Square North, and Louisa May Alcott penned *Little Women* just a few streets away.

After a decade of construction, New York's Grand Central Terminal was completed in 1913. Here, amid the grandeur of Beaux Arts detailing, trains and subways on several levels whisk travelers in and out of the city.

The 1,046-foot Chrysler Building, a beautiful example of art deco styling, was the tallest in the world for only a few months in 1930 before the Empire State Building eclipsed it. More interesting than its height is the Chrysler Building's gleaming stainless-steel façade. Triangular windows decorate seven arches, narrowing to a final spire.

Both Chicago and New York claim to be the birthplace of the skyscraper. Whether or not it was first, New York quickly embraced the new steel-framed buildings, and the towers of the city skyline climbed higher and higher throughout the early 1900s.

New York's thriving movie industry is second only to that of Los Angeles.
A site like this one, where technicians set up for a scene in Chelsea, is an
opportunity to spot a movie star or glimpse the inside workings of a set.

From roller rinks and boxing rings to rock-climbing walls and driving ranges, Chelsea Piers on the Hudson River offers many recreational options. At the golf club, enthusiasts can have their swings video-analyzed, practice their putting on a 1,200-square-foot green, or perfect their chipping at the indoor sand bunker.

Built in 1902, Daniel H. Burnham's Flatiron Building combined new technology—including the use of steel frames—with historical appeal. This building once marked the end of the "ladies' mile," a collection of shops and boutiques, and is still a great place for shopping.

King Kong fell from it, in 1945 a B-25 bomber crashed into its 79th floor, and lightning strikes it 500 times a year: the Empire State Building is firmly ensconced in the history and mythology of New York City.

More than 117 million people have taken one of 73 elevators up the 1,250-foot Empire State Building, to gaze at the panoramic views from observatories on the 86th and 102nd floors. Competitors in the Annual Empire State Building Run Up use an alternate route—climbing 1,575 steps from the lobby to the 86th floor each spring.

In the 1920s, John D. Rockefeller envisioned a bustling commercial district in midtown Manhattan and hired three architectural companies to achieve that goal. The result is Rockefeller Center, 19 commercial buildings occupying 11 acres. In winter, a skating rink is created below the sculpture and it is very popular with tourists and locals.

Atlas stands with the world on his shoulders in Rockefeller Center. When Lee Lowrie and Rene Chambellan unveiled their statue in 1937, the work was surrounded by protestors. It seems the figure's face resembled that of Italian dictator Mussolini.

In CBS's Ed Sullivan Theater, David Letterman performs to live audiences and late-night TV watchers across the continent. The show moved to this Broadway location in 1993.

Named for the *New York Times* offices, built here in 1904, Times Square is one of the city's most famous venues. Whether destined for offices, Broadway plays, or restaurants, more than 1.7 million people pass through each day.

Along with restaurant signs and theater marquees, 25 "super-signs" light Times Square, known as the Crossroads of the World.

A venue for many concerts and festivals, and an afternoon escape for city workers, Bryant Park is one of the city's favorite destinations.

53

Radio City Music Hall was the world's largest indoor theater when it opened
in 1932. The Rockettes first performed here a year later. Having hosted
300 million guests—more than 10 times the population of New York—
the theater has recently undergone a massive $70-million restoration.

New York's oldest cathedral, St. Patrick's has inspired awe in visitors since its dedication in 1815. The Roman Catholic church is home to an 1868 pipe organ. The cemetery outside is the resting place of past bishops and Civil War soldiers.

For more than a century, Carnegie Hall has hosted some of the world's most famous dancers, speakers, and musicians. Tickets for opening night in 1891 cost up to $2.00, and New York's finest families—including the Rockefellers—were in attendance.

Saks Fifth Avenue, founded by Andrew Saks, opened its doors in 1924. Shoppers at the posh department store—one of the most famous in the world—can have their parcels delivered directly to their Manhattan hotel rooms.

From Tiffany and Saks to Christian Dior and Versace, Fifth Avenue offers shoppers the best of everything. Taxi drivers, renowned for their aggressiveness, whisk shoppers through the streets.

At Bloomingdale's (Bloomie's, if you're a local), a personal shopper can help you find the perfect Chanel dress and specially trained beauty consultants can spritz you with the latest Calvin Klein perfume. The store has been enticing shoppers since 1927.

Whether you're a fan of Elvis or AC/DC, you'll find enough rock and roll memorabilia at the Hard Rock Café to entertain you long after you've finished your signature burger.

Frederick Law Olmsted designed Central Park as a green oasis where city dwellers could escape. About 15 million people a year do just that, wandering the paths of the 840-acre preserve.

The roads in Central Park close to traffic on weekends, and in-line skaters take to the pavement. From wobbly beginners to experienced skaters, all sorts of enthusiasts flock to the park. And many come here just to watch.

About 20,000 workers helped reshape the landscape of Central Park when it was designed in the late 1800s; in the process, more gunpowder was used than at the Battle of Gettysburg.

Carriages capture the romance of New York in any season. Central Park was first proposed by local families who had admired landscaped parks in Paris and London. A park in New York, they argued, would allow them to take family Sunday carriage rides, and would keep workers out of pubs.

As attendance at Central Park boomed in the early and mid-1900s, city leaders saw a need for more recreational facilities. Playgrounds, a skating rink, a pool, boathouses, and playing fields were added.

Made famous by the movies, the lake in Central Park is the perfect place to rent a rowboat, hire a gondolier to ply the waters, or enjoy the view from the famous Bow Bridge.

69

The Metropolitan Museum of Art, better known as The Met, boasts two million pieces of art from around the world. The first object in the collections was a Roman sarcophagus, acquired just after the museum was founded in 1870.

Some historians believe that wealthy families turned to selling apples on the streets of New York during the depression, earning the city its nickname The Big Apple. Others say the term was first used by jazz musicians, referring to a booking in New York as a big success.

From earliest dinosaur discoveries to the newest space technology, the 42 permanent exhibits of the American Museum of Natural History cover vast realms of information. Visitors can wander from the rainforest to the moon in just a few minutes, or spend hours poring over artifacts from ancient North America.

Harlem was named in the seventeenth century by Dutch governor Peter Stuyvesant after the Dutch city of the same name. The neighborhood became mainly African American in the early 1900s. Author James Arthur Baldwin, civil rights activist A. Philip Randolph, and singer Billie Holiday lived here, and Malcolm X died here in 1965.

Spanning 15 acres, Lincoln Center is the world's largest cultural venue. The brain-child of philanthropist John D. Rockefeller, the center is the headquarters for the Metropolitan Opera, the New York Philharmonic, the Juilliard School of Music, and the New York City Ballet, and hosts countless other performance groups each year.

Thousands of works
by modern masters,
from Kandinsky and
Klee to Picasso and
Van Gogh, are housed
in the Solomon R.
Guggenheim Museum,
designed by Frank
Lloyd Wright. This is
New York's youngest
designated landmark.

Reminiscent of a New England fishing village, City Island is home to a collection of cafés and seafood restaurants. Sailboats and yachts line the docks, and sunbathers laze on the public beach.

A sailboat catches the wind on the Hudson River, the skyline of Manhattan behind it. The river is named for English explorer Henry Hudson, who sailed from the coast upriver to Albany in 1609.

Wooden bleachers originally accommodated the fans at Yankee Stadium. Seating was expanded in 1927 and again in 1938. Today, the stands can hold over 57,500 people.

The popularity of baseball in New York boomed after Babe Ruth began hitting home runs, and Yankee Stadium opened in 1923 to accommodate the new crowds. In the years to come, players such as Lou Gehrig, Yogi Berra, and Reggie "Mr. October" Jackson also thrilled spectators.

More than 12,000 plant species flourish at the Brooklyn Botanical Gardens. In the late 1800s, this area was an ash dump. Thanks to a decision by New York State in 1897 to reserve 39 acres for a botanical garden, the site now includes blooms from around the world.

Brooklyn was first linked to New York by the Brooklyn Bridge in 1883, and residents still think of themselves as citizens of a separate city. Brooklyn Heights, with its picturesque promenade, is one of the borough's most fashionable neighborhoods.

The Brooklyn and
Manhattan bridges
span the East River.
Manhattan is flanked
by three rivers—the
Hudson on the west,
the Harlem on the
north, and the East
River to the east.

After Frederick Law Olmsted and architect Calvert Vaux won fame
for their design of Central Park, the city of Brooklyn invited them
to create Prospect Park. Part of the Battle of Long Island was fought
here during the War of Independence.

Though faded since its time as a famous seaside resort in the early 1900s, Coney Island's amusement park atmosphere still attracts thrill seekers and sun lovers.

Staten Island remained a rural retreat long after New York was a booming metropolis. The island drew more residents after the Verrazano Narrows Bridge opened in 1964. Now both bridge and ferry shuttle commuters.

The Staten Island Ferry is as much tourist attraction as transportation option. Locals and visitors alike can't help but stare at the Manhattan skyline as the ferry glides through the Upper Bay.

Built in 1909, the Queensboro Bridge spans the East River between Manhattan and the borough of Queens, first settled by English home-steaders more than three centuries ago.

Actual firefighters lead tours through the New York City Fire Museum, a refurbished fire hall that features water buckets, hand pumps, fire carriages, lanterns, and lifesaving nets from the city's past.

The Unisphere in Flushing stands as a reminder of the 1964 World's Fair. The steel structure was created to symbolize peace between nations around the world.

Long, narrow Manhattan has been called a basking trout surrounded by four lily pads—the other boroughs. Together, they encompass 300 square miles, some of the most densely populated land in the nation.

94

Photo Credits